LOW ROAD WEST™

PHILLIP KENNEDY JOHNSON · FLAVIANO · MIQUEL MUERTO

BOOM! Studios, 5670 Wilshire Boulevard, Suite 400, Los Angeles, CA, 90036-5679. Printed in China. First Printing.

ISBN: 978-1-68415-374-9, eISBN: 978-1-64144-357-9

WRITTEN BY
PHILLIP KENNEDY JOHNSON

ILLUSTRATED BY
FLAVIANO

COLORED BY
MIQUEL MUERTO

LETTERED BY
JIM CAMPBELL

COVER BY
FLAVIANO

SERIES DESIGNER
MARIE KRUPINA

COLLECTION DESIGNER
KARA LEOPARD

ASSISTANT EDITOR
GAVIN GRONENTHAL

EDITOR
ERIC HARBURN

LOW ROAD WEST™

CREATED BY PHILLIP KENNEDY JOHNSON & FLAVIANO

"THERE IS NO DEATH...ONLY CHANGE.
AND NOWHERE IN THE UNIVERSE
IS THAT MORE TRUE THAN HERE."

—FROM THE JOURNALS OF
DOCTOR ABRAHAM MORROW, 1873

CHAPTER ONE

I-40 W
Amarillo 166
Albuquerque 452

I-40 W
SCHOOL BUS
166
452
STOP WHEN
RED LIGHTS FLASH

I-40 W
Amarillo 166
Albuquerque 452
CLICK
YOU ARE ON
LOW ROAD WEST.

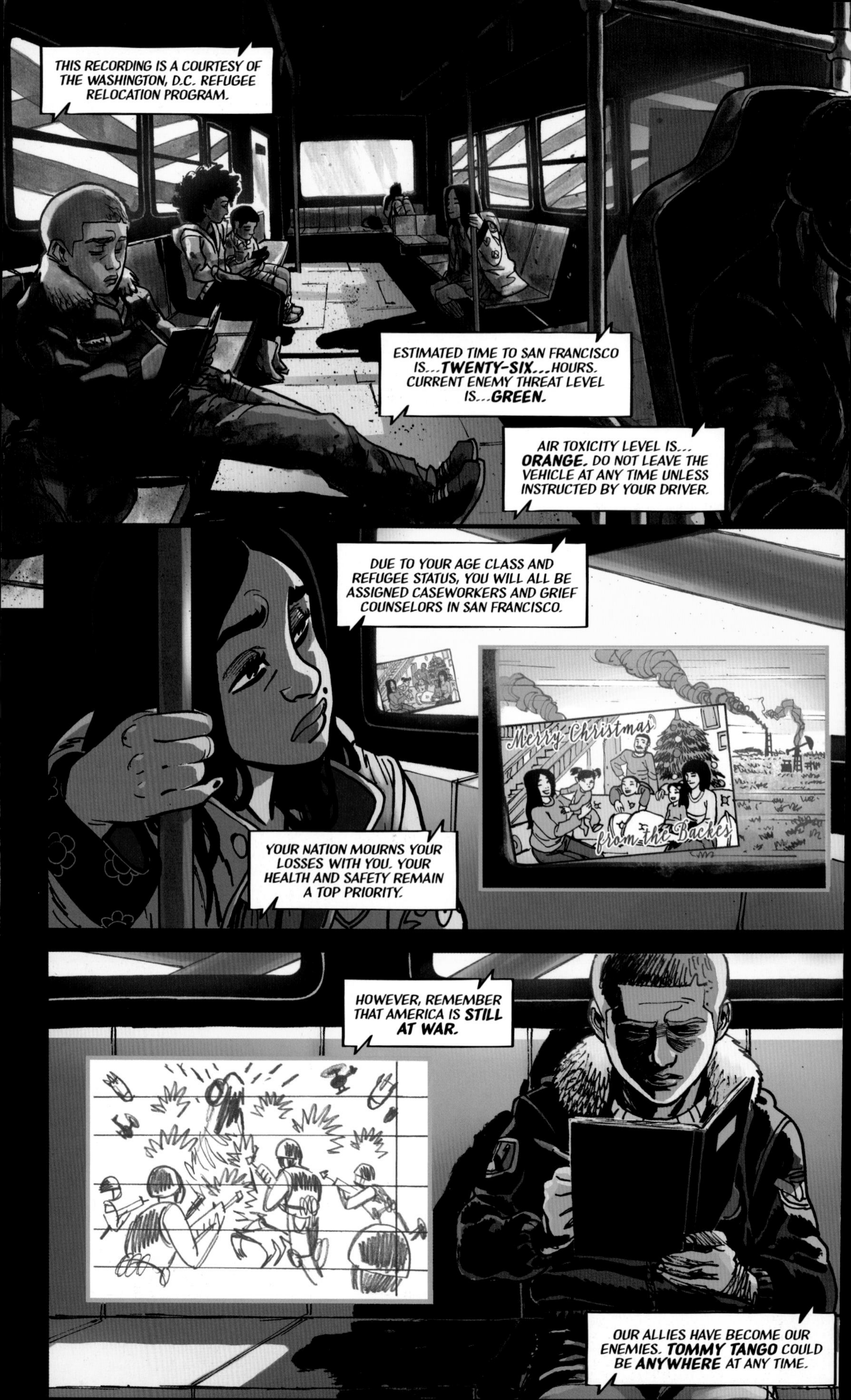
THIS RECORDING IS A COURTESY OF THE WASHINGTON, D.C. REFUGEE RELOCATION PROGRAM.
ESTIMATED TIME TO SAN FRANCISCO IS... TWENTY-SIX... HOURS. CURRENT ENEMY THREAT LEVEL IS... GREEN.
AIR TOXICITY LEVEL IS... ORANGE. DO NOT LEAVE THE VEHICLE AT ANY TIME UNLESS INSTRUCTED BY YOUR DRIVER.
DUE TO YOUR AGE CLASS AND REFUGEE STATUS, YOU WILL ALL BE ASSIGNED CASEWORKERS AND GRIEF COUNSELORS IN SAN FRANCISCO.
Merry Christmas
from the Backes
YOUR NATION MOURNS YOUR LOSSES WITH YOU. YOUR HEALTH AND SAFETY REMAIN A TOP PRIORITY.
HOWEVER, REMEMBER THAT AMERICA IS STILL AT WAR.
OUR ALLIES HAVE BECOME OUR ENEMIES. TOMMY TANGO COULD BE ANYWHERE AT ANY TIME.

DO NOT TRUST THE PEOPLE AROUND YOU. DO NOT SHARE SENSITIVE INFORMATION OR DETAILED PERSONAL ACCOUNTS.
IF A PASSENGER LOOKS SUSPICIOUS OR MAKES UNWARRANTED CONVERSATION, ALERT YOUR DRIVER IMMEDIATELY.
CONGRATULATIONS ON YOUR ENROLLMENT IN THE REFUGEE RELOCATION PROGRAM.
WE HOPE LOW ROAD WEST IS YOUR DOOR TO A NEW LIFE.
MORE THAN EVER, YOU ARE THE FUTURE OF THIS GREAT NATION!
ERRNNNK
KCHNK
KCHNKK

STAY SAFE...STAY VIGILANT...
AND STAY LOYAL!
CLICK
WHY ARE WE STOPPING?
RRRRNK
RRRRRNNNK
CHANK FSSSSHHH

HEY!

WHAT ARE YOU DOING?
ARE YOU LEAVING US?!
MDW LRW-30

SCHOOL BUS
STOP WHEN RED LIGHTS FLASH
YOU-YOU CAN'T! WE HAVE TO GET TO SAN FRANCISCO!
MY BROTHER'S ONLY TEN, HE WON'T MAKE I OUT HERE!

WAIT!

WHAT THE HELL...?
YOUR GAME LOOKS COOL.

YOU'RE PLAYING DOORS, RIGHT? WHERE YOU BUILD MAGIC DOORS OUT OF STUFF?

ONE OF MY SISTERS LIKED THAT ONE.

LIKES IT, I MEAN. HAHA.
SHE GOT OUT, SHE'S IN CHICAGO. SHE'S NOT, YOU KNOW... DEAD, OR ANYTHING.

WHAT'S YOUR NAME?
UH... GUYS?

I THINK WE'RE IN TROUBLE.
DOES ANYBODY KNOW HOW TO DRIVE?!

...WHAT?
OUR DRIVER JUST LEFT US!
I DON'T EVEN SEE ANY **KEYS!**
WHAT DO YOU MEAN, HE ***LEFT*** US?!
THAT IS...***REALLY*** NOT GOOD. HOW LONG SINCE WE SAW ACTUAL PEOPLE?
HOURS! PROBABLY TWO HUNDRED MILES.
OH MY GOD THIS ISN'T HAPPENING
YEAH, WE'D NEED A WEEK TO WALK THAT.
WALK?! THE RADIO SAID NOT TO LEAVE THE BUS!
AND PHONES DON'T WORK OUT HERE, ALL THE TOWERS ARE DOWN.
WHAT FOOD AND WATER DO WE HAVE?
UM...I HAVE A LITTLE VITAMIN WATER LEFT.
AND PART OF AN ATKINS BAR.
UH, YOU ARE ***NOT*** GETTING MY BROTHER'S FOOD.

WHAT ABOUT BATTERIES? I HAVE A FLASHLIGHT. WHAT KIND OF BATTERIES DOES HIS GAME--
HE NEEDS HIS GAME, TOO.
QUEEP QUIRP
ARE YO ***SERIO*** RIGH NOW?
ARE ***YOU?***

WHY WOULD I NOT PRIORITIZE MY BROTHER OVER A BUNCH OF STRANGERS? SORRY, NOT SORRY.
OH, WOW.
WHERE DID YOU COME FROM?
WE NEED TO KNOW WHAT RESOURCES WE HAVE! WE NEED FOOD, WATER, WEAPONS IN CASE TOMMIES COME...
OH MAN, ARE YOU ONE OF THOSE? WHY WOULD "TOMMIES" BE ALL THE WAY OUT HERE?
YOU NEVER KNOW.

HEY. YOU'RE OVER SIXTEEN, RIGHT?
DO YOU KNOW HOW TO DRIVE A BUS?

NOT ONE THAT'S OUT OF GAS.

HEY!
WHERE ARE YOU GOING?
DOES IT MATTER? WE CAN'T STAY HERE.
C'MON, WE NEED TO STAY TOGETHER.
WE'RE NOT SUPPOSED TO LEAVE THE BUS!
I HAVE TO PEE.

COUGH
WHY IS THE AIR LIKE THIS?
PRETTY MUCH EVERY OIL WELL IN THE U.S. IS ON FIRE.
BRUSH FIRES BURN OFF VEGETATION QUICKER THAN IT CAN GROW. HALF OF THE MIDWEST IS DESERT NOW.
THERE'S NOTHING TO HOLD DOWN THE SOIL, SO WHEN THE WIND BLOWS IT ALL GOES FLYING, LIKE A SANDSTORM.
WOW, YOU KNOW A LOT ABOUT DESERTS.
IS THAT SUPPOSED TO BE FUNNY?
WHOA! WHERE DID THAT COME FROM?
YEAH, SHE DIDN'T EVEN DO ANYTHING!
I-IT'S OKAY.
I'M SORRY IF I SAID SOMETHING DUMB.
LET'S JUST STOP TALKING.
WE NEED TO SAVE MOISTURE ANYWAY.

WHAT IS THIS?
OLD MILITARY CHECKPOINT. THEY USED TO BE ALL ALONG THE REFUGEE CORRIDORS.

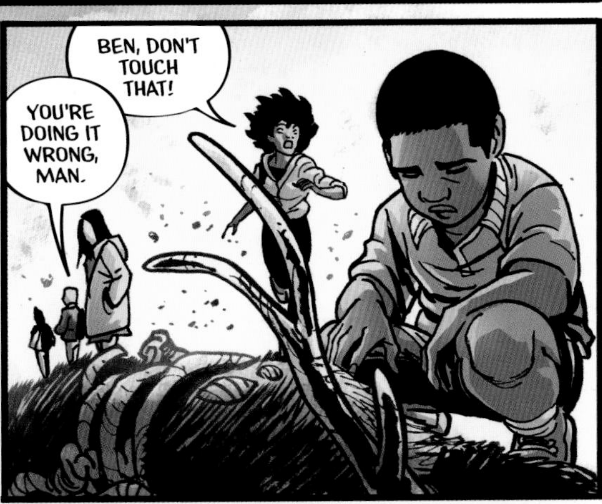
EW, GROSS.
MY DAD TOLD ME ABOUT THIS STUFF.
BEN, DON'T!
HE'S AN ARMY RANGER. McQUEEN AY-EFF.

REALLY? BUT...IF YOU STILL HAVE A DAD, HOW DID YOU GET ON A REFUGEE BUS?
BECAUSE HE'S LYING. ALSO, WE SHOULD FIND SHELTER BEFORE THE DUST STORM HITS US.

BEN, DON'T TOUCH THAT!
YOU'RE DOING IT WRONG, MAN.

TOMMY TANGOS ARE SUPPOSED TO TRICK AMERICANS INTO *LIKING* THEM. MAKES IT EASIER TO BETRAY US, SEE?
GEE, I WONDER WHY YOU THINK I'M AN ENEMY. RACIST MUCH?
JERK MUCH?
WHY DON'T YOU--

BLEEEEHHH

WHUH... WH-WHAT'S HAPPENING?!
BLEEGEGEH

GET AWAY!

KACRACK

BEN, NO!
WHAT JUST HAPPENED?!
DID YOUR BROTHER DO THAT?

NO! HE JUST...H-HE HAS A THING FOR DEAD ANIMALS!
NO! THAT WASN'T HIM!
A THING WHERE HE BRINGS THEM TO LIFE?!
WHY DID HE EVEN TOUCH IT?

LOOK, WE'VE SEEN SOME STUFF, ALL RIGHT?!
HE PLAYS WITH DEAD ANIMALS SOMETIMES. I THINK HE'S TRYING TO FIGURE OUT WHAT DEATH...IS, OR SOMETHING.

BOY, HAS HE COME TO THE RIGHT PLACE.

HEY THERE.
WHERE'D Y'ALL COME FROM?
COME ON, CARL, LOOK AT 'EM. THEY'RE REFUGEES. MUSTA RUN OUTTA GAS.
WE SEEN SOME OTHERS WHO RAN OUTTA GAS. AIN'T A FULL PUMP FOR A THOUSAND MILES OUT HERE.
WH-WHAT WAS WRONG WITH THAT DEER?
AND WHERE ARE WE?
WOW. I DON'T LIKE KIDS, BUT THIS IS KIND OF ADORABLE.
YEAH, WE GOT SOME BAD NEWS FOR YOU BUNCH.
WHY? HOW FAR IS THE NEXT TOWN?
THERE AIN'T NO *"NEXT TOWN,"* KID. THIS IS THE END OF THE LINE.
YOU JUST WANDERED INTO ***DUSTER'S WAKE.***

THIS BUNCH LOOKS A LITTLE SOFT FOR REFUGEES.
DOUGHY, EVEN.
I DON'T KNOW, LITTLE MAN LOOKS KINDA HARD.

HOW 'BOUT IT, LITTLE MAN? YOU A HARD CASE?
YUH...YEAH. HELL YEAH. WE'RE FROM WASHINGTON.
WASHINGTON, D.C.?! LAST WE HEARD, FIGHTING WAS CRAZY UP THERE! YOU MUSTA SEEN SOME MESSED-UP $#!%, HUH?

Y-YEAH. MY DAD'S SPECIAL FORCES. KICKS ALL KINDS OF TOMMY ASS.
I WANTED TO STAY AND HELP FIGHT, BUT THEY MADE US EVACUATE. SUCKS.

HAHAHA! LITTLE MAN, YOU ARE HARDCORE.
THINK WE SHOULD BRING HIM ON THE CREW?

NOPE.
I THINK WE SHOULD TAKE ALL THEIR STUFF AND BEAT 'EM TO DEATH.

OH MAN, LOOK AT THIS!
DON'T TOUCH THAT!
CRACK
LEAVE HER ALONE!
SKIP TO THE END, CARL, STORM'S ROLLING IN!
I KNOW WHAT YOU ARE! YOU'RE DESERTERS!
OKAY, IT'S NOT CUTE ANYMORE.
MY DAD IS GONNA KICK YOUR ASS STRAIGHT TO HELL!
DON'T TAKE IT SO HARD, LITTLE MAN.
NOTHING STAYS DEAD AROUND HERE.

THWIPP
YAAAUUGH!
WHFFF
TUNK
SHE'S HERE!
FIND HER!
AAAAAUUUGGH!
GET YOU, YOU LITTLE BITCH
...WHAT HAPPENED?
THERE'S SOMEONE ELSE OUT THERE!
BEN, COME ON!
LEAVE THE STUPID GAME!

WHERE ARE WE GOING?
JUST KEEP MOVING!
?
WHAT?!
THERE'S A HOUSE!
BAM
HURRY, GET IT SHUT!
SLAM

WHOA.
UM...
...THIS HOUSE WASN'T THIS BIG FROM OUTSIDE.
FROM THE ROAD, THERE WEREN'T ANY HOUSES.
SSSH... SSH, IT'S OKAY...
=SNIFF= WE'LL FIND YOU A NEW ONE.
IT WASN'T JUST A STUPID GAME! IT WAS...HIS ESCAPE, YOU KNOW?
WE LOST OUR...OUR PARENTS, AND HE SAW...AND IN HIS GAME, HE COULD MAKE DOORS, AND WORLDS... AND HE COULD PRETEND--

MY NAME'S ANGELA.
HE'S BEN.
I'M EMMA.
SHAWN.
AMIR.

THIS HOUSE IS SO UNBELIEVABLY McQUEEN.
SSH.
WHAT DOES THAT *MEAN?*
WHY ARE YOU SHUSHING ME?
I AM NOT.
YOU'RE BEING ANNOYING.
QUIPP
QUEEP QUIRRRUP
WHOA.
WAS THE LAST OWNER A MAD SCIENTIST, OR A... GANDALF?
I'LL PRETEND YOU DIDN'T JUST SAY "A GANDALF."
OH MY GOD, IS THAT A HUMAN SKULL OVER THERE?
HOLY CRAP.
"TAKE A LOOK AT THIS."

NONE OF THIS WAS HERE BEFORE.
WHERE'S THE ROAD?!
WHAT IF THEY WERE RIGHT?
ARE WE TRAPPED HERE? LIKE... FOREVER?
I'M NOT READY TO ACCEPT THAT.

"I DON'T PRETEND TO UNDERSTAND THIS PLACE. IT'S OBVIOUSLY BEEN PRETTY...UNPREDICTABLE."
OH, YOU THINK? THE DEAD THINGS COMING TO LIFE PART, OR THE CREEPY MAGIC GHOST TOWN PART?
LISTEN... WE'RE STUCK WITH EACH OTHER, ALL RIGHT?
WASHINGTON'S STILL GETTING BOMBED. MOST OF US SAW OUR FAMILIES DIE. NOBODY IS LOOKING FOR US.
"BUT AT LEAST WE'RE NOT ALONE."
THOSE DESERTERS ARE SURVIVING OUT HERE. IF WE START TRUSTING EACH OTHER A LITTLE, WE CAN TOO.
LOW ROAD WEST CAN STILL BE...WHAT WAS IT THE PROPAGANDA RECORDING CALLED IT?
OUR "DOOR TO A NEW LIFE."
OH MY GOD.
"WHERE'S BEN?"

"BEN, WHERE ARE YOU?!"

ISSUE TWO COVER BY
FLAVIANO

CHAPTER TWO

I BET MY TOES FALL OFF.
HEH. THAT'D BE WEIRD-LOOKIN'.
GOD, THIS HURTS LIKE A SONOVABITCH.
HEY. HEY HEY.
WHAT?
YOU HEAR SOMETHING?
LIKE WHAT?
LIKE...A MOTORCYCLE.
HEAR IT? IT JUST CUT OFF.
PLEASE. LIKE ANYBODY'D BE ON A BIKE IN THIS--
SCREEEK
HOLY DAMN.

IT'S CHRISTMAS MORNING.
OLD MAN, YOU JUST WALKED INTO THE WRONG--
AW, SON.
SHRIPPP
I WISH YOU HADN'T.
SPLOSH

SORRY, SON. I KNOW IT HURTS.
BREATHE REAL SLOW AND DEEP, LET IT BLEED OUT. IT'LL BE OVER IN A LITTLE WHILE.
YOU BOYS KNOW WHO I AM?
I-I DO.
THEN YOU KNOW I'M NO FRIEND TO DESERTERS.
BUT I'M HERE ON GOVERNMENT BUSINESS, AND I WOULDN'T SAY NO TO SOME LOCAL HELP.
ANY KIDS COME THROUGH HERE TODAY?

BEN!
BEN?
HE WOULDN'T HAVE GONE OUTSIDE, WOULD HE?

BE--

OH MY GOD, BEN!
WE FOUND HIM!
WHY DIDN'T YOU ANSWER? WHAT WERE YOU DOING?

The bones sent me away.
BONES? AWAY WHERE?
There were people there. Not like us... big, and quiet.
I lost my bird, so I stayed with them for a long time.
The sky is shiny red, like pennies.
want to see?
WAS THAT SIGN LANGUAGE? WHAT'S HE SAYING?
...NOTHING.
HE'S NOT SAYING ANYTHING.

BEN... BEN, WAIT.
WHY SIGN LANGUAGE? HE'S NOT DEAF.
AFTER OUR PARENTS DIED, HE STOPPED TALKING. I DIDN'T KNOW REAL SIGN LANGUAGE, SO WE MADE UP OUR OWN.
WHAT WAS HE SAYING?
IT DIDN'T MAKE ANY SENSE. SOMETHING FROM HIS OLD VIDEO GAME, MAYBE.
SOOOO, THERE'S NO FOOD OR WATER IN THE HOUSE.
IT SOUNDS LIKE THE STORM'S LETTING UP...WE SHOULD SEARCH THE OTHER BUILDINGS BEFORE IT GETS DARK.
ARE YOU SERIOUS?! THOSE DESERTERS ARE STILL OUT THERE!
HEY, WE NEED STUFF. WE HAVE TO GO OUT SOMETIME.
ANYBODY ELSE COMING?
I CAN'T LEAVE BEN. HE'S BEEN ACTING WEIRD, I'M AFRAID HE MIGHT RUN AWAY.
I WANT TO START GOING THROUGH THOSE JOURNALS UPSTAIRS. I BET THERE'S STUFF ABOUT THIS TOWN THAT WILL HELP US.
I'LL GO.
YOU SHOULDN'T GO BY YOURSELF.

WHOA.
"DUSTER'S WAKE."
DUSTER'S WAKE
IT LOOKS LIKE A... CREEPY VIDEO GAME, OR SOMETHING.
THAT'D BE SWEET, ACTUALLY. EVERY TIME WE KILLED A ZOMBIE, FOOD OR AMMO WOULD POP OUT OF IT LIKE A PIÑATA.
CLANK
AND THE BOSS FIGHT WOULD DEFINITELY BE IN THERE.

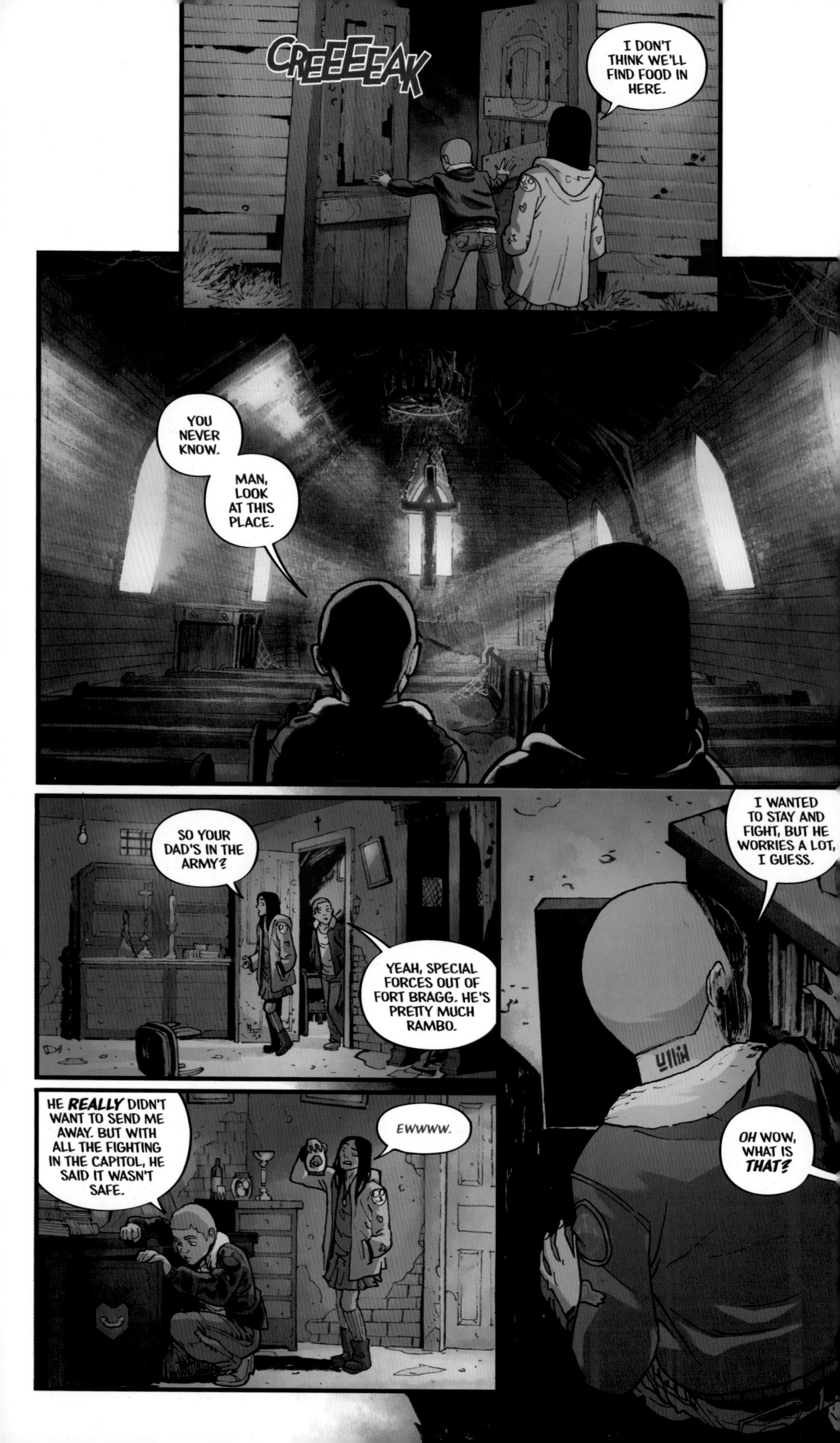
CREEEEAK
I DON'T THINK WE'LL FIND FOOD IN HERE.
YOU NEVER KNOW.
MAN, LOOK AT THIS PLACE.
SO YOUR DAD'S IN THE ARMY?
YEAH, SPECIAL FORCES OUT OF FORT BRAGG. HE'S PRETTY MUCH RAMBO.
I WANTED TO STAY AND FIGHT, BUT HE WORRIES A LOT, I GUESS.
HE REALLY DIDN'T WANT TO SEND ME AWAY. BUT WITH ALL THE FIGHTING IN THE CAPITOL, HE SAID IT WASN'T SAFE.
EWWWW.
OH WOW, WHAT IS THAT?

DO YOU HAVE A *TATTOO* ON YOUR NECK?
WHAT? NO, I-I DON'T HAVE ANY TATTOOS.

OH. I THOUGHT I SAW...
NO, THAT'S... IT'S NOT A TATTOO.
ANYWAY, WHAT ABOUT YOU? WHAT HAPPENED TO YOUR FAMILY?

OH, THEY ALL GOT OUT. MY DAD'S, LIKE, ***REALLY*** IMPORTANT. HE GOT MY FAMILY ON A SECRET PENTAGON PLANE OR SOMETHING.
I WAS SUPPOSED TO GO TOO, BUT THERE WAS A BOMBING BY MY SCHOOL AND ALL THE STREETS SHUT DOWN.

OH. YOU, *UM*... YOU HEARD FROM THEM AFTER THAT? I THOUGHT THE AIRPORTS ALL GOT--
NO, THEY'RE ALL FINE.
IT'S OKAY, THOUGH. THEY'RE IN CHICAGO, THEY'RE FINE.

SNIFF
UM...
...THAT'S GREAT. I'M GLAD THEY MADE IT OUT.

I BET WHEN WE GET TO SAN FRANCISCO, IT'LL BE EASY TO HOOK BACK UP WITH THEM.
LISTEN... I DIDN'T MEAN TO--
SNIFF YEAH, TOTALLY.
GRRRRRR

GRRRRRRRRRR
OKAY... WE'RE OKAY. JUST DON'T SHOW FEAR.
WHATEVER YOU DO, DON'T...
...RUN.

RRRROWROWROW

ROWROWROWRO
ARK
ARK
ARK AR

GET IN THE TRUCK!
ARKARK
GRR

SLAM
KKSSSSH
ROWROWROW
ARK ARK ARK ARK
THEY'RE GETTING IN!
GRROWWW
THEY'RE NOT GONNA GET IN!
ARK ARK ARK
SHAWN, I'M SORRY!
THEY'RE NOT GETTING IN!
I'M SORRY I RAN, I--
GRRRRRRRR
YIKE
THOCK
YIKE YIKE
YIKE
YIKE
YIKE

YOU MUSTA TRIPPED ONE OF MY "DINNER BELLS." THEY MAKE THE DOGS COME.
WHO ARE YOU?
CLANK
TUNK
UM... SHAWN.
I'M ANGELA.
MY NAME'S HARM.
WANNA SEE SOME STUFF I MADE?

OH. HI.
FOUND SOME OLD PENCILS?
HEY...
...I JUST THOUGHT OF SOMETHING.
THIS LOOKS LIKE SOMETHING MY BROTHER SHOWED ME ONCE.
CLICK
CLICKCLICK
HA! I THOUGHT SO. IT'S A THREE-DIMENSIONAL RIDDLE!
THE BIRD SINGS A MELODY FRAGMENT, DICTATED BY ITS SHAPE.
AND IF YOU MOVE THE PIECES AROUND, CHANGING ITS SHAPE...
...THE MELODY CHANGES, OR GROWS LONGER! HERE, TRY TO--

GIVE IT BACK!
I WAS!
YEAH, BECAUSE YOU TOOK IT!
I WAS SHOWING HIM HOW IT WORKS!
YOU KNOW WHAT? SCREW THIS.
I HAVE READING TO DO. GO PLAY WITH YOUR TRASH SOMEWHERE ELSE.
LISTEN...I'M REALLY SORRY I HURT YOUR FEELINGS BEFORE.
IF I HAD TOLD THEM WHAT YOU SAID ABOUT MAGIC BONES AND COPPER SKIES, THEY WOULDN'T HAVE BELIEVED US.

I WAS THINKING MAYBE WE COULD PLAY TOGETHER IN YOUR...COPPER SKY PLACE.
WOULD YOU LIKE THAT?

HAHA, HEY! I CAN'T KEEP UP!

THIS IS MY PLACE!
OH, RAD.
THIS IS SO McQUEEN! DID YOU MAKE ALL THIS STUFF?
UH-HUH! WITH ALL THE BROKE CARS AROUND, I USED TO TRY TO PUT ONE TOGETHER THAT MOVED, BUT THEY NEVER DID.
NOW I MOSTLY JUST MAKE THINGS I LIKE.
THAT WAS YOU WHO SHOT THOSE DESERTERS BEFORE, RIGHT?
THE ROBBERS? UH-HUH. THEY'RE NOT SUPPOSED TO BE HERE, BUT THEY GOT TOO CLOSE AND NOW THEY'RE STUCK, LIKE YOU.
"STUCK"?
HOW LONG HAVE YOU BEEN HERE?
HOW LONG? THAT SOUNDS WEIRD.
HOW LONG? LIKE... YOU KNOW, HOW LONG? WHEN DID YOU GET HERE?
YOU SAY DUMB THINGS.
BURRRRRRRRRUHP.

HARM, PLEASE. THIS IS IMPORTANT. WE NEED TO GET TO SAN FRANCISCO.
HOW FAR IS THE NEAREST TOWN?
TOO FAR. TOOOOOOOO FAR, TOO FAR.
WITH ALL THE JUNKERS AROUND HERE, THERE'S NOT ONE WORKING CAR?!
WOULDN'T MATTER. DUSTER'S WAKE DOESN'T LET PEOPLE LEAVE.
IT'S BENDY.
"BENDY"? WHAT DOES THAT MEAN, "BENDY"?
IT DOESN'T LIKE PEOPLE TO LEAVE.
WHEN YOU TRY...
IT JUST GOES ALL BENDY.

IS THAT THE SCIENTIFIC TERM?
EVERYBODY TAKE IT DOWN A NOTCH! I'M ONE OF THE GOOD GUYS.
COLONEL JIMMY HARPER, MILITARY DISTRICT OF WASHINGTON. SOME FOLKS JUST CALL ME "THE COLONEL."
SEE, THE GOVERNMENT SENDS ME OUT ON... SPECIAL CASES. THAT'S WHAT YOU ARE, SHAWN.
HA! SURPRISED? THAT'S RIGHT, I KNOW YOU.
YOU TOO, ANGELA. EVERYONE WHO WAS ON THAT BUS. SPECIAL CASES, ALL.
BUT I'M REALLY ONLY INTERESTED...

"...IN ONE OF YOU."
May 2nd, 1873.
The climate in Custer's Wake is intolerable.
Lily should murder me in my sleep for dragging our family to such a desolate place...
...THE BASEMENT AGAIN? WE CAN'T PLAY DOWN HERE, BEN, IT'S TOO DARK!
PRETTY SURE THERE'S NO COPPER SKY DOWN--
--OH MY GOD.
...but there has never been a nobler scientific pursuit than the one that called me here.

Already, the implications of what I have found are unthinkable.
WE-WE SHOULDN'T HAVE COME HERE. WE DON'T KNOW WHO COULD...
QUIRP
QUIRREEP
Simply put: the world is not as we believed it to be.
The constancy of three-dimensional space...
...the linear passage of time...
BEN?! WHAT--
...the inevitability of death.
Not constants, but variables.
If I am right about what lies under the ground, my work may reconcile a central tenet of both science and faith:
at there no death.
Only CHANGE.

And nowhere in the universe is that more true than here.
—Doctor Abraham Morrow

ISSUE THREE COVER BY
FLAVIANO

CHAPTER THREE

My relationship with religion has been on-again, off-again since my days as an altar boy.
But it gave me one gift that I have held close my entire life:
The notion that nothing ends.
For me, it is a much grander, more profound idea than any belief or disbelief in gods or devils.
I hold to the knowledge, the CERTAINTY that life is a form of energy that goes on forever.
If I had any doubt before, this place would have wiped it away in an instant.
Here, under a copper sky...

...I have found the meaning of "eternity."
—from the journals of Doctor Abraham Morrow, 1873
BEN!
BEN, WHERE ARE Y--

riously, these phenomena grow more radical
e closer they occur to two points:
he salt flats just east of the Custer mine—which
he Indians call "The Wail"—and the late Tom Custer's
ouse, where my own family now sleeps.
You may not think your new companions as clever as your brother...
...but they have qualities and capabilities that may surprise you.
and capabilities that
In time, they could fill the void left by your family.
WHAT THE...?!
In time, they could fill the void left by your
What happened with your brother was not your fault, Amir.

AAAHH!
WHAP
WHO... WHO ARE YOU?
WHERE ARE YOU?
My name is Abraham.
I am in a place I call Copper Sky.

WHERE ARE WE GOING?
down. home.
HOME?
YOU AN GET E BACK OME?
down.
home.

YOU NEVER TOLD ME HOW YOU KNOW OUR SIGN LANGUAGE. **NOBODY** KNOWS IT, EXCEPT ME AND BEN.
DO YOU HAVE MIND POWERS OR SOMETHING?

AND WHY ISN'T **BEN** HERE?
WE WERE HOLDING HANDS WHEN WE GOT... SUCKED IN, OR WHATEVER. BUT I GUESS HE DIDN'T CROSS OVER.

I SHOULD PROBABLY BE GRATEFUL. HE WOULDN'T LAST TWO SECONDS OVER HERE.

HUFF
HUFF IS THIS HUFF WHERE WE'RE GOING?

WOW. OKAY.
YOU HAVE SOMETHING DOWN HERE THAT WILL SEND ME HOME?
Home.
WAIT... THIS IS *YOUR* HOME?!
NO, NONONONO! I HAVE TO GET BACK TO *MY* WORLD, *MY* HOME! MY BROTHER NEEDS ME, I HAVE TO GET *HOME!*
WE *ARE* HOME, SIS.

WHAT TOOK YOU SO LONG?

BAHMANI...?
AHMED BAHMANI WAS THE D.C. DEFECTOR. HE LEAKED INTEL THAT OPENED UP THE EAST COAST TO INVASION.
AHMED WAS AMIR'S BIG BROTHER. AND NO MATTER WHAT THE MEDIA SAID, HE WAS NOTHING BUT A TRAITOR. WORST WE EVER HAD.
WHOLE WORLD'S JUST US AND THEM NOW, LITTLE MAN. WE NEED A WIN ON THE BOARD.
WHERE'S THE BAHMANI KID?
BUT... AHMED BAHMANI'S DEAD.
AMIR'S A JERK, BUT... HE'S NOT HIS BROTHER, RIGHT?
WE DON'T ARREST PEOPLE BECAUSE OF WHO THEIR FAMILY IS. NOT IN AMERICA.
RIGHT?

I GUESS I SHOULDN'T BE SURPRISED.
AH-AH. NOT A CHANCE.
DROP IT.
CTANK
TLINK
CLANNNG
CLANNNG
TELL ME, "SHAWN"...WHAT HAPPENED TO THE REAL SHAWN? IS HE STILL ALIVE?
DID HE EVEN KNOW HE'D LOST HIS EVAC PAPERS BEFORE HE GOT TO THE STATION?

MAYBE THEY ASSIGNED HIM YOUR SPOT ON THE CAPITAL ROAD CREWS, SINCE YOU RAN AWAY AND ALL.
SHAWN?
WHAT'S HE--
AGK...!
THE ROAD CREWS ARE IMPORTANT, "SHAWN." OUR BOYS NEED THOSE ROADS CLEAR.
YOU THINK THAT'S NOT WORTH A LITTLE RADIATION SICKNESS? A FEW DEAD HOMELESS?
OU'RE NO PATRIOT.
JUST ANOTHER LOW-LIFE ESERTER, LIKE YOUR OLD MAN.
THE KIND OF TRASH WHO'D SELL HIS OWN SON TO THE CREWS FOR A TICKET OUT OF--
GRRRRR
RRRRRRRRRRRRRRR
?
WHAT THE HELL WAS THAT?!
DINNER BELL.

GRRRAAAAAAA
AAAHH, GET BACK!
GRRRRRRRRR
N-NO... NO, BAD DOG!
YAAAAUUGH!
GRROWWFF
FWIPP
THOCK
GRRRRRRRRR
ROWROWROW

GET OFF!
SHAWN!
WHUMP

-HUFF- ARE YOU GUYS OKAY?
Y-YEAH, COME ON!

GRRROWFF

BWHOOOOM

BWHOOOM
AAAAHH... AAAAHH!
I-I THINK I'M HURT REAL BAD!
NOT AS BAD AS SOME ARE GONNA BE.

THIS ISN'T REAL.
THIS ISN'T POSSIBLE.
HOW ARE YOU DOING THIS?!
ARE YOU THE ONE WHO WROTE THESE JOURNALS? THEY'RE LIKE A HUNDRED YEARS OLD, HOW ARE YOU NOT DEAD?
There is no death. Only change.
ARE YOU THE ONE WHO BUILT THAT PUZZLE? THE RIDDLE BIRD?
There is no death. Only change. You need to leave, Amir. The THIN MAN is coming.
KKSSSH
BWHOOM

HE'S SHOOTING AT US!
YOU THINK?!
WAIT.
YOU'RE GOING IN **THERE?!**
THAT'S WHERE THE OTHERS ARE!
THAT... THAT'S **HOLLOW HOUSE.** I CAN'T GO IN THERE.
IF YOU STAY, HE'LL KILL YOU!
COME ON!

HOW...
HOW?
THE FIRST TIME I CROSSED, I WAS HERE A LONG TIME.
HOW LONG?
TIME DOESN'T GO IN STRAIGHT LINES HERE. IT SPEEDS UP, SLOWS DOWN...HOLDS STILL, SLIPS SIDEWAYS.
IS THIS... WHAT I THINK IT IS?
HAHA, YEAH. THE BIRD ANGELA GAVE ME.
I DON'T THINK IT CAN CROSS INTO COPPER SKY ON ITS OWN, BUT IT CAN DEFINITELY CROSS BACK. SAVED MY BUTT THE LAST TIME.
AND WHAT ABOUT... THEM?
I CALL THEM THE SHEPHERDS. THEY FOUND ME THE FIRST TIME I CAME. WE TAKE

LIKE FAMILY, YOU MEAN?
EMMA...
BEN, WHY DID YOU BRING ME HERE?
BECAUSE OF WHAT'S COMING.
WHAT'S COMING?
THE SHEPHERDS CALL IT THE GODSLINGER. AND THEY BELIEVE IT'LL BE THE END OF ALL WORLDS.
WHAT'S IT GOT TO DO WITH US?
EVERYTHING.

YOU, SIR...

...ARE **CHANGIN'.**

ISSUE FOUR COVER BY
FLAVIANO

CHAPTER FOUR

BWHOOM
WHO ARE YOU?
I'M THE ONE OWNS THIS PLACE. YOU'RE THE TRESPASSER.
WHY CAN'T I SEE YOU?
BECAUSE I'M EVERYWHERE AND EVERYTHING.

H-HEY...DO YOU GUYS HEAR SOMETHING?
THOSE'RE MY DOGS YOU SHOT, JIMMY HARPER.
YOU KEEP WHAT YOU KILL AROUND HERE.
I AIN'T GONNA HURT YOU, THOUGH. LIKE AS NOT, WE NEED EACH OTHER.
NEED EACH OTHER.
SURE. BIG THINGS COMIN', JIMMY.

YOU AND ME, WE'RE GONNA DO BIG THINGS TOGETHER.

WHAT IS THAT?!
THAT'S THE PANTHEON. A FAMILY OF GODS THAT COME TO COPPER SKY SOMEDAY.
HALF OF THE SHEPHERDS' STORIES REVOLVE AROUND THEM.
YOU SAY "THEM" LIKE THEY'RE NOT US!
THIS SCULPTURE WAS HERE WAY BEFORE I GOT HERE. THEY'VE BEEN EXPECTING US.
IN SOME STORIES, THE PANTHEON COMES TOGETHER TO MAKE GREAT THINGS, OR TO FIGHT POWERFUL THREATS. IN OTHERS, THEY FIGHT BETWEEN THEMSELVES.
THEY MAKE MOUNTAINS, AND RIVERS, AND ARMIES, AND CONTINENTS.
THEY BUILD A CIVILIZATION, AND AFTER IT RISES UP AGAINST THEM, THEY BUILD ANOTHER ONE.

THEY CALL THAT ONE THE GUARDIAN.
THE PROPHET.
THE WARRIOR.
THE SCHOLAR.
AND THE TRICKSTER.
"THE TRICKSTER," HUH?
DOESN'T LOOK MUCH LIKE ANGELA.
WHAT'S THAT ONE, WAY OVER THERE? IS THAT...?
NO. THAT'S THE MAKER.
I'M NOT CONVINCED THAT ONE EXISTS.

YOU SAID THERE'S SOMETHING BAD HERE... SOMETHING CONNECTED TO US.
THE "GODSLINGER"?
TO UNDERSTAND THE GODSLINGER, YOU NEED TO KNOW HOW DEATH WORKS HERE.
HERE, DEATH ISN'T THE END.
"HERE, WHEN YOU TAKE A LIFE, YOU LITERALLY TAKE IT.
"IT BECOMES PART OF YOU, AND THE STRONGEST PARTS OF BOTH MAKE SOMETHING NEW.
"ON THE DAY WE ALL COME TO COPPER SKY, SOMETHING EVIL FOLLOWS US. IT KILLS SOMETHING BIG, OR MAYBE SOMETHING BIG KILLS IT.
"EITHER WAY, THEY BECOME SOMETHING NEW."
AND IT GROWS SO POWERFUL THAT CONSUMES THIS WORLD. MAYBE EVEN ALL WORLDS.
BEN, HOW CAN YOU POSSIBLY KNOW--
TIME IS DIFFERENT HERE, EMMA. THESE THINGS HAPPEN. THEY'VE ALREADY HAPPENED. THEY'RE HAPPENING NOW.
IF OUR FRIENDS COME HERE, THE GODSLINGER FOLLOWS.
WE CAN'T LET THEM FIND THIS PLACE.

BWHOOM
THAT SHOT WAS CLOSER.
THERE'S A LOT OF BUILDINGS... WHOEVER'S SHOOTING, THEY CAN'T KNOW ANYONE'S IN THIS HOUSE, COULD THEY?
If you stay here, you'll die, Amir.
WHAT, I'M SUPPOSED TO JUST LEAVE THE OTHERS?!
No. You wouldn't survive the storm.
THEN WHAT?!?
The bones are a door.
Find the bones.

BAM
WHOA...!
YOU SCARED THE CRAP OUT OF ME! WAS THAT YOU SHOOTING?
AND WHO'S THIS?!
WHUHH!
SHAWN!
CRACK
WHAT THE HELL IS WRONG WITH--
THEY SENT A FRACKIN' COMMANDING SECURITY OFFICER AFTER YOU! YOU COULD'VE TOLD US!
YOU COULD HAVE TOLD US YOUR BROTHER WAS THE TERRORIST WHO BLEW UP THE WORLD!

WHY WOULD I TELL YOU ANYTHING?! WHAT ABOUT YOU, AND ALL THAT SUPER-DAD B.S.?!
YOU'VE GOT A CAPITAL ROAD CREWS TAG ON YOUR NECK!
WHERE WAS SUPER-DAD WHEN YOU WERE ENSLAVED BY YOUR OWN MILITARY, CLEARING BODIES AND RAD-WASTE OFF THE STREETS SO TANKS COULD GET THROUGH?
YOU ONLY END UP ON THE CREWS IF YOU'RE HOMELESS, OR IF YOUR PARENTS SELL YOU!

I WASN'T GOING TO SAY ANYTHING. I FELT SORRY FOR YOU.
I'VE GOT NO IDEA HOW YOU EVEN GOT AWAY, LET ALONE HOW YOU SCORED A SEAT ON A REFUGEE BUS.

BUT DON'T YOU TALK TO ME ABOUT HONESTY, OR TELL ME I SHOULD BE ASHAMED OF MY BROTHER, BECAUSE I'M NOT!
MY BROTHER WAS A CHEMICAL ENGINEER! HE WAS A GENIUS!

AND HE LOOKED OUT FOR ME!
DID YOUR DAD LOOK OUT FOR YOU?!

ARE YOU OKAY?
YOU DON'T LOOK GOOD.
BWHOOM
WE NEED A PLACE TO HIDE.
WHAT ABOUT THE BASEM--
NO.
I KNOW A BETTER PLACE.

BEN?
WHEN WE GET BACK, WILL YOU BE LITTLE AGAIN?
I GUESS SO. THAT'S WHAT HAPPENED LAST TIME.
I STILL MIGHT NOT BE ABLE TO TALK. I'LL REMEMBER THE THINGS THAT HAPPENED HERE, BUT... I WON'T JUST BE MY OLDER SELF IN A YOUNG BODY.
I GUESS WHAT I MEAN IS...
...YOU'LL STILL NEED ME, WON'T YOU?
AFTER MOM AND DAD DIED... IF I HADN'T HAD YOU TO TAKE CARE OF...
...I STILL NEED YOU TO NEED ME, OKAY?
PLEASE?
WE'LL ALWAYS NEED EACH OTHER.

NO.
THERE SHOULD BE A STAIRCASE HERE!
YOU SAID YOU KNEW THIS HOUSE!
IT'S GOING BENDY! WHEN WE LIVED HERE, THE ATTIC STAIR WAS RIGHT--
YOU *LIVED* HERE?!
DO YOU KNOW ABOUT ABRAHAM? OR COPPER SKY? DO YOU KNOW WHAT *"FIND THE BONES"* MEANS?
I...
...HOW DO YOU...

OH.
HI.

WAS THAT...
WERE YOU IN COPPER SKY?
HOW DO YOU KNOW ABOUT COPPER SKY?
WAS ABRAHAM THERE?
WHO?
I CAN'T.
EVERYONE, THIS IS HARM. HARM, BEN, EMMA.
WHAT? NO. ARE WE NOT GOING TO TALK ABOUT THIS?
CRASH
NO TIME NOW.
THEY'RE INSIDE.

June 23rd, 1873.
Tom Custer came to own this land through the most underhanded of means.
He married a woman of the Cheyenne tribe, and stole the land out from under them.
-SNUFF-
He built his mine and used the Indians as miners, promising them "ownership stakes" rather than money.
His Indian wife mostly kept to herself.
She stayed inside more and more, until she was scarcely ever seen, even by her own family.
When the Indians discovered he had killed her and buried her in the cellar...

...things went very
badly for him.
—Doctor Abraham
Morrow, 1873
CLUNK
THIS JUNK DON'T BELONG HERE.
THIS HOUSE WAS MINE.
WHEN A MAN DIES, THEY OUGHTA PUT HIM IN THE GROUND WITH EVERYTHING HE OWNS.
KIDS... HORSES... WOMEN... DOGS...
...EVERY DAMNED THING.
WHATEVER DON'T FIT, STACK IT ALL UP IN HIS HOUSE AND BURN IT TO THE GROUND.
NO OTHER MAN'S GOT ANY RIGHT TO IT.

END OF THE HALL, UP THE STAIRS.
THIS DOESN'T MAKE SENSE.
WE'VE BEEN PRETTY MUCH HEADING WEST FOR-**EVER!** WE SHOULD BE HUNDREDS OF YARDS OUTSIDE THE HOUSE BY NOW!
I TOLD YOU, THIS PLACE GOES ALL **BENDY!**
WHEN WE FIND THE ATTIC, WE CAN LOCK OURSELVES INSIDE.
ABRAHAM SAID OUR ONLY WAY OUT IS TO FIND THE BONES.
YOU KNOW WHAT THAT MEANS, DON'T YOU?
A-ABRAHAM'S DEAD.
AND I AM **NOT** GOING DOWN THERE A--
THOK
WHOUFFF!
GONNA KILL YOU, TOMMY...

GONNA DO WHAT I--
WHACK
BY THE AUTHORITY OF THE UNITED STATES GOVERNMENT...
...YOU ARE ALL UNDER ARREST.
COME ON!
TUNNNG
SWIFF
BWHOOM

KTCH
UNF!
SHUT THE DOOR!
SLAM
CRUNCH
WHAT THE HELL...?!
OVER THERE!

WHAT...?

WH-WHAT JUST--
"BENDY"?
UH-HUH.
SLAM
I GUESS IT DIDN'T WANT THEM TO COME.
WE NEED TO FIND THE BASEMENT! THE BONES ARE DOWN THERE, THEY'RE THE DOOR!
I'M SORRY, BEN.
I WON'T LET YOU DIE FOR SOME STUPID PROPHECY.
HAHA.

WE MIGHT... MIGHT NOT HAVE A CHOICE ANYMORE.
HAHA.
DON'T ANY OF YO SMELL IT?
OH NO.

NO
NO NO NO
NO

NO!
BEN, WE HAVE TO!
WE CAN'T GET THROUGH!
WELL, HOLY DAMN.

IT'S CHRISTMAS MORNING.

ISSUE FIVE COVER BY
FLAVIANO

CHAPTER FIVE

END OF THE LINE, YOUNGSTERS.
YOU'VE ASSAULTED AN OFFICER IN THE U.S. ARMY, AND SEVERAL ENLISTED MEN BESIDES.
GET YOUR HANDS OFF MY BROTHER!
FWHIPP
SPLURK
KACRACK
AAAAAHH!
I CALL THAT RUDE.
GROOAAAAAANNN

KAKOOOOOOM
CRAASSSSH
KREEEEE CRACK
CRAAASSH

CRASH
OUFFFF
AAHH!
WHUMP
LOOK OUT!
DEAD.
DEAD, DEAD, DEAD.
...!

I KNEW IT.
I KNEW IT SINCE I FIRST TOOK SHOVEL TO SOIL.
KNEW THERE WAS SOMETHIN' UNDER THE SURFACE, BLEEDIN' INTO MY TOWN, MAKIN' IT UNNATURAL.

CUSTER'S WAKE IS A DOOR.
WHEN I LAID MY CLAIM TO THAT MINE...
I LAID CLAIM TO A WHOLE WORLD.
HM.
INDIANS WHEREVER YOU GO.
I DON'T KNOW WHAT YOU'RE SAYIN', REDSKIN...
...BUT IT SURE SOUNDS LIKE A THREAT TO ME.
NO!

HRUKK
WHAT'S WRONG WITH HIM?
KEEP... WHAT YOU KILL.
RUN!
HURRK

IF WE GET FAR ENOUGH FROM THE OTHERS, THE BIRD CAN SEND US BACK AND TRAP THEM HERE!
WHAT ABOUT STOPPING THE GODSLINGER?

STOPPING WHAT?! WHAT HAPPENED BACK THERE?
WE CAN'T STOP IT NOW! IT'S ALREADY HAPPENING!

WHEN YOU KILL SOMETHING HERE, IT BECOMES PART OF YOU! AND IF YOU KILL SOMETHING REALLY BAD, OR STRONGER THAN YOU...
...JUST DON'T.

ARE YOU OKAY?
YOU DON'T NEED TO BE SCARED. YOU'RE, LIKE, OUR ONLY BAD-ASS.
NOT SCARED OF THEM.

SCARED OF THIS PLACE. BAD THINGS HAPPEN HERE.
WELL, DON'T BE SCARED.

BEN AND I WON'T LET ANYTHING BAD HAPPEN TO YOU.
NOT TO ANY OF US.
YAAAAAAHHHH!

SMASH
THIS WON'T GO LIKE BEFORE, LITTLE MAN!
NO ONE'S BAILING YOU OUT THIS TIME!
WE'RE FASTER.
STRONGER.
SPLORTCH!
BETTER.
SHAWN!
WAIT YOUR TURN.
SHFFF
WHUNK
ABRAHAM... WHERE ARE YOU? YOU TOLD ME TO COME HERE! WE NEED YOU!
HELP US!

No.
I don't have the power to change any of this, Amir. These pages were written before you were born.
SWIFF
I didn't bring you here because you need me.
I brought you here because THEY will need YOU.

THOCK
YAAAAGGGHH!

WHOA! YOU HURT IT!
WHAT WAS--
HIS GUN!

ANGELA... REMEMBER WHAT HE DID TO HIS GUN?
TIME WAS...

...A CHILD HAD THE GOOD SENSE NOT TO HARM A MAN'S DOGS.
DOGS ARE DAMNED USEFUL.

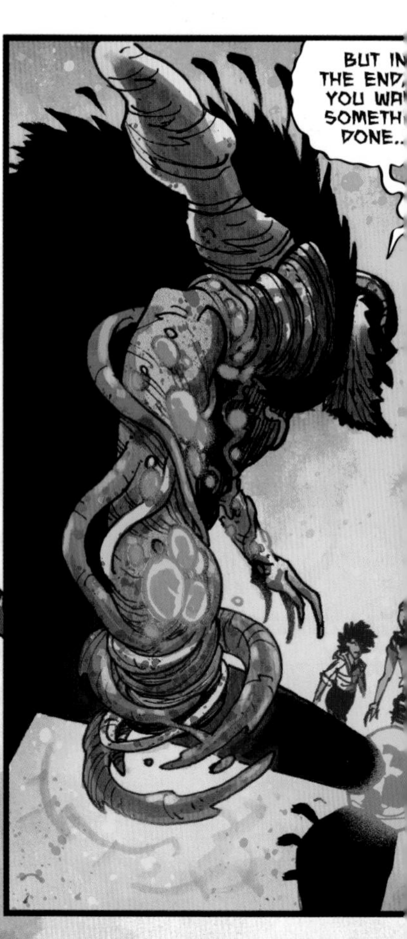

...DO IT YOURSELF.
BAWHOOOOOOM

YOU'RE THE GODSLINGER.
YOU... YOU KILLED YOUR OWN PEOPLE.
YOU KIDS THINK DEATH'S AN EVIL, BUT IT AIN'T.
DEATH MAKES YOU **STRONG.** ESPECIALLY HERE.
YOU THINK TOM CUSTER DIED ALL THOSE YEARS AGO? YOU THINK I KILLED THEM TWO BOYS JUST NOW, OR THOSE MEDICINE MEN?
NO, SIR. I'M ***ALL*** THOSE THINGS NOW.
AND I'LL BE A LOT MORE.

GRRRAAAALLLOOO
SOON, I'LL BE ALL THERE IS.
THOOOOOM
ANGELA! THE ARROW!
REMEMBE HIS GUN!

I CAN HEAR THEM ALL, BOYS. ALL INSIDE MY MIND.
INSIDE MY SOUL, IF THERE IS SUCH A THING.
I WONDER WHAT YOU'LL SOUND LI--
SSSHLUNK
--LI...

SHRRRRRIPPP
...ANGELA?
NO! YOU SHOULDN'T HAVE KILLED--
IT'S OKAY. NONE OF THIS IS REAL.
IT'S ALL GOING TO BE OKAY NOW.
ANGELA, NO! RUN!

ANGELA!
GET OUT OF THERE!
WHUFFF
KRAKOOOOOOM
NNOOOOOOOOO!
...A-ABRAHAM?

BEN...
N-NO... NO NO NO NO!
IT'S GONNA BE OKAY. YOU'RE GONNA BE OKAY.
THIS IS WHAT...WHAT SHE WANTED. JUST TO PROTECT YOU. TO PROTECT ALL OF US.
YOU'RE GONNA BE O--
NO! THIS ISN'T HOW IT WAS SUPPOSED TO BE! EMMA'S SUPPOSED TO BE HERE, WITH BEN!
I'M SUPPOSED TO BE WITH MY BROTHER AND SISTERS! TH-THEY NEED ME TO READ TO THEM!
MOM READS WHEN I'M NOT THERE, BUT SHE DOESN'T DO IT RIGHT!
YOU'RE GONNA BE OKAY.
PLEASE...
...I JUST WANT TO GO HOME!

TWO WEEKS LATER.

SZOCK!
WHOA. DID I GET IT?
FINALLY.
YOU'RE TOO BREATHE-Y WHEN YOU SHOOT.
HEH.
SO...NOW WHAT?
SKIN IT AND GUT IT, BEFORE THE FLIES MAKE FLY-BABIES.
PAT PAT
HAVE FUN WITH THAT.

ARE YOU SURE YOU DON'T WANT TO STAY IN THE HOUSE WITH--
YYYYEP.
EVEN AFTER THE FIRE, IT'S TWICE AS SAFE AS ANY OF THE OTHER--
NOOOOPE.
WELL, JUST EAT WITH US, THEN.
JUST HELP YOU GUT YOUR CRITTER, YOU MEAN?
...MAYBE.
HRM.
FINE, I GUESS.
IS SHE GONNA COME TOO?
UM... HEY.
I THINK WE'RE GONNA TRY COOKING IN A BIT. ARE YOU HUNGRY?
I'M GOING TO STAY HERE FOR A WHILE.

ANGELA... ARE YOU OKAY? EVER SINCE WE CAME BACK, YOU'VE BEEN--
"CAME BACK"? CAME BACK FROM *WHAT?*

A BUNCH OF SHELL-SHOCKED REFUGEES WITH DEAD FAMILIES FIND A MAGICAL WORLD WHERE DEATH DOESN'T EXIST?
YOU KNOW HALLUCINATIONS ARE PART OF *PTSD*, RIGHT?

IT WASN'T REAL, **"SHAWN."**
OR WHATEVER YOUR NAME IS.
...
IT **WAS** REAL. AND WE STILL NEED EACH OTHER.
NEED EACH OTHER...
...YEAH...
...GONNA DO BIG THINGS TOGETHER.

DO YOU THINK THE BIRD GOT HER OUT IN TIME?
DO YOU THINK SHE'S STILL HER?
I JUST HOPE SHE'S ONLY HER.
BEN?
BEN! COME HELP US SKIN A PRAIRIE DOG!
LOOKS LIKE THIS DELICIOUS TREAT IS ALL FOR US.
I WONDER WHERE BEN IS.
HOUSE PROBABLY ATE HIM.
WHY ARE YOU SO AFRAID OF THIS PLACE? DIDN'T YOU SAY YOU USED TO LIVE HERE?
IT'S FINE. YOU DON'T HAVE TO TELL US.
TALK ABOUT IT WHEN YOU'RE READY.
Abraham Paul Melody Harmony Lily

THERE'S A WELL IN BACK. FIND A PITCHER.
I GUESS YOU'VE BEEN IN DUSTER'S WAKE A LONG TIME, *HUH?*
THIS MUST BE CRAZY FOR YOU.
WHAT?
HAVING A FAMILY AGAIN.
I'VE BEEN MEANING TO ASK...IN COPPER SKY, I SAW THAT GUY ON THE RIDGE.
YOU LOOKED LIKE YOU KNEW HIM.
THINK THAT WAS ABRAHAM.
WHO'S ABRAHAM?
A SCIENTIST WHO FOUND COPPER SKY A LONG TIME AGO. HIS JOURNALS MAKE IT SOUND LIKE HE GOT TRAPPED OVER THERE.
WHAT DO THEY SAY?
...A LOT OF THINGS.

"MOSTLY, THEY SAY THERE ARE NO ENDINGS.
"EVEN DEATH ISN'T THE END. NOT THE WAY WE PERCEIVE IT TO BE.
"THE DEAD ARE CHANGED, THE KILLER IS CHANGED, THE ENVIRONMENT CHANGES...BUT NOTHING ENDS.
"EVEN HERE.
"BUT ESPECIALLY IN COPPER SKY."

ISSUE ONE COVER BY
DAVID LAFUENTE

ADDITIONAL ARTWORK BY **FLAVIANO**